MARY BAKER EDDY

A Life from Beginning to End

Copyright © 2019 by Hourly History.

All rights reserved.

Table of Contents

Introduction
The Divine Calling
Healed by Prayer
Early Love and Loss
The Issue of Slavery
Separated from Her Son
Mary during the American Civil War
The Birth of Christian Science
On the Brink of Death
A Matter of Faith
Conclusion

Introduction

Mary Baker Eddy stands unique in our collective remembrances of supposed prophets of the bygone past. She was a girl that quite literally felt a calling at an early age when she thought she heard a divine voice call her name. Shortly thereafter she was intermittently beset with chronic illnesses and remarkable bouts of healing. Mary Baker Eddy did not claim to understand where her spontaneous remissions were coming from until much later in life; it was in old age, when no one expected Mary Baker Eddy to do much of anything except retire, that she entered into her great final act, and in doing so, she rocked the entire religious world to its core.

Whether or not you believe her claims of healing and divine intervention, the story of Mary Baker Eddy, founder of the Church of Christ, Scientist, is a riveting one all the same.

Chapter One

The Divine Calling

"Reject hatred without hating."

—Mary Baker Eddy

The girl named Mary Morse Baker—the name of "Eddy" by which her future followers would know her would be added later—was born in Bow, New Hampshire on July 16, 1821 to a farmer by the name of Mark Baker and his spouse Abigail Barnard Baker. From the very start, Mary was part of a family of strong faith and conviction. Her father Mark was a Protestant Congregationalist who often preached fire and brimstone at the family dinner table. According to Mary's later recollection, discussions about judgment and eternal damnation were just as common growing up as hearing someone say "pass the potatoes."

The Baker family was big; Mary had five older siblings, and all of the children regularly helped out on the family farm where they each had their role to fill. Although their father was loving, he was also quite a stern taskmaster. As such, the children were expected to rest only on the day of the Sabbath. Despite his hard work ethic, Mark strictly believed in the biblical day of rest, and if he caught anyone working on this day, he would become quite irate. Apparently, when it came to the observance of the

Sabbath on the Baker farm, even the farm animals were expected to comply as was dramatically indicated on one occasion when Mary's father allegedly beat a bird to death with his cane for "for hoppin' about on the Sabbath." This was the world of very real religious conviction and extreme austerity in which Mary Baker Eddy would come to cut her spiritual teeth.

Mary's New Hampshire roots ran deep. Her father Mark's farm in Bow was already well established at the time of her birth, having been cultivated by her grandfather many years before. In this home, Mark attempted to instill his rock-solid sense of order, but Mary proved to be a little more resilient to his commands than the other children. In fact, there were some instances in which this youngest child openly rebelled against her parents.

Shortly before she passed away, Mary reminisced with her close friends about one time as a small child when her father was taking too long to finish praying for the family. Growing weary of the loud and repetitive invocations of her father, Mary reached for one of her mother's sewing needles while everyone else's eyes were closed and gave her father the surprise of his life. Right when he was in the middle of his passionate oratory, she crept up behind him and poked him in the back with the needle. This blatant disruption of prayerful devotion is certainly at odds with Mary's later life of religious dedication, but it also bears testament to the strong-willed streak of determination with which Mary was endowed.

Despite her previous irreverence to her father's prayer sessions, Mary would soon find that she herself would be called forth by a higher power. Mary would later claim that when she was just eight years old she could hear the call of God. Initially, she was confused when she heard this utterance and mistook this voice to be that of her mother. Mary allegedly went to her mother to ask her what she wanted, but her mother denied calling upon her, yet Mary persisted, saying, "I heard someone call Mary three times!"

Mary would continue to claim that she heard a voice calling her name over the next three years. Even though the idea of auditory hallucinations was not very well understood in those days, Mary's parents soon grew concerned for her mental health. Mark seemed to be under the impression that the young Mary had been wearing her mind out by spending too much time with her books. He felt that in her voracious studies she was overtaxing herself, or as he stated at the time, "Take the books away from her—her brain is too big for her body!"

Mary's parents did indeed feel that she had been spending too much time alone reading books and soon ordered her to go outside to play in the fields. But even after she spent more time playing outside, the little girl still felt that something beyond human experience was attempting to communicate with her. Rather than just being all in Mary's mind, there were occasions in which those around her claimed to have heard the voice as well. One of Mary's cousins, a girl named Mehitable Huntoon, would later recall that as children, during one of their

family get-togethers, they both heard disembodied voice calling Mary's name. ?
initially thought it was Mary's mother calling .
told her, "Your mother is calling you!"

Prompted by her cousin, Mary then repeated the routine that had become quite common in those days. She went to her mother and asked why she called her, only for her mother to say that it was not she who issued the call. Abigail was now getting tired and frustrated with what she initially thought was a mere child's game, but when Mary's cousin confirmed that she had heard it too, Mary's mother began to wonder. Finally, considering that perhaps there really was something to it, Abigail opened her Bible and read to Mary the story of the biblical prophet Samuel who according to scripture had been similarly called by God. Abigail, now entertaining the idea that there might be a supernatural basis for the happenings, advised her child to answer the call with, "Speak, Lord, for thy servant heareth."

Mary tried to take these words to heart, but the next time she heard the voice, she became frightened and remained silent. Having missed her opportunity, Mary felt awful and cried out to God for forgiveness for her actions. Whatever was happening to young Mary, she felt sincerely distraught that she had failed to accept the call that she supposedly had been given.

Mary heard the voice again beckoning her shortly thereafter, and this time she did indeed summon the courage to answer it just as her mother had directed her. But strangely enough, as soon as she answered in this manner, the voice ceased to speak and, according to Mary, never spoke again. This moment would stick with Mary for the rest of her life. No matter what happened, she never ceased to believe that she had a true calling in her life.

Chapter Two

Healed by Prayer

"Disease is an experience of a so-called mortal mind. It is fear made manifest on the body."

—Mary Baker Eddy

At the time that Mary was obtaining her basic education of reading, writing, and arithmetic at a nearby schoolhouse, most of her older siblings were already either entering or getting ready to enter the workforce. The oldest Baker child, Samuel, had left for the city of Boston to pursue the craft of masonry, and the second oldest, Albert, had left home in order to study at Dartmouth College. Mary's other siblings weren't very far behind in ascending the ladder of responsible adulthood. That left Mary as the only remaining child of the family, still learning the ropes in life. As such, she was often the center of attention at home with the constant care of her mother and the rigid authority of her father shaping her outlook.

Although Mark Baker could seem harsh and overbearing, Mary came to admire and respect her father's fair sense of judgment. Mark was often made a local arbiter of disputes in the community, and within this framework Mary saw her father's steely logic at work. If two local farmers had an argument concerning their properties, for example, Mark Baker would usually find a way to diffuse the situation. There was one occasion, however, in which Mark was unable to find a solution to the woes of the homesteaders, and Mary herself was inspired to step into the fray. It is said that as one of the men angrily debated her father's findings, Mary rose to the occasion. Imitating words she had heard her father say countless times in the past, she quietly asked the agitated farmer, "Mr. Bartlett, why do you articulate so vociferously?" The remark sounded so odd coming from the little girl that everyone in attendance immediately erupted in laughter, forgetting all about their previous tension and animosity. The men then came to terms with each other and left the Bakers with their problems resolved. Mark would proudly acknowledge Mary's role afterward, stating, "Mary settled that quarrel."

Besides her parents, another guiding light for Mary in her childhood was the local pastor of their church, Pembroke Burnham. Pembroke would often stop by at the family farm to have animated conversations with Mary's father about important issues concerning the church and the world at large. Mary was amazed at how the pastor would rant on and on about backsliding parishioners and the coming Apocalypse. For young Mary, the fire and brimstone of the itinerant preacher's words were not necessary to get her on her knees in prayer. By the age of ten, she was already praying seven times a day. She is said to have done this as a kind of homage to the figures of the

Bible, such as Daniel and David, whom she very much adored.

During these prayer vigils, Mary was also sure to keep a diary of the contents of her daily supplications. She did this so she could examine what was on her heart during the prayers and that way gauge her spiritual growth from day to day. In many ways, the writings of Mary's prayer journals began to take on the form of a biblical prophet. Many biblical prophets did indeed record their prayers in like manner, producing some of the works of the Bible in the process.

It seems that all of this religious fervor would reach a crossroads for young Mary when she was 12 years old. It was at this time that Mary's firmly held belief in a loving and redemptive God came into conflict with her father's belief in predestination. Mark Baker was an adherent to the doctrinal idea that the final fate of the souls of humanity is something that is determined before those souls are even born. In other words, the decision as to whether someone is going to heaven or hell is predetermined before that person incarnates into this world. This was not an idea that Mary could entertain; she believed that the hearts of men could be changed with a little effort on the part of the faithful.

It was also at age 12 that Mary allegedly first began to feel the power of prayerful healing, which would later become a cornerstone of Christian Science. Mary was often weak and sickly as a child, frequently bedridden with fevers. It is alleged that during one of these episodes, she was able to pray the fever away. This event would create a lifelong search for the healing power of Christian Science.

Chapter Three

Early Love and Loss

"Spirit is the real and eternal; matter is the unreal and temporal."

—Mary Baker Eddy

The first major change in Mary Baker Eddy's life occurred in 1836 when she was 15 years old and her father decided to leave their ancestral farm behind and move to a new homestead in Sanbornton Bridge, New Hampshire some 20 miles away. In doing this, the title to the farm was given over to Mark Baker's nieces and nephews.

Mary's brothers had moved on at this time, and so Mary shared her parents' new home with her 18-year-old sister Martha and 20-year-old sister Abigail. Here, in their new settings, the Bakers became something akin to local socialites, holding regular get-togethers with members of the community. Mary's father was also fast becoming an important fixture of the church, holding regular meetings with the clergy.

Mary attended school at the Holmes Academy in Plymouth, beginning in 1838, and later completed her education at Sanbornton Academy. She was known as a bright student and a fast learner by both her teachers and her peers, although towards the end of Mary's life some of her classmates would have some rather unflattering things to say about her. One classmate, in particular, by the name of Page Philbrook had some rather unkind words and remembrances. Years after Mary was already famous for her theological efforts, Philbrook stated that Mary "held herself superior to the children and would not join their games" and that she was "idle and backward in her lessons, and sat through the school hours scribbling, and would pretend to be ill when she was not."

Much of this can be written off as gossip, but the claim that Mary feigned illness is one that would follow her throughout her life. Some detractors would later claim that those miraculous cases in which Mary healed herself occurred only because she was never sick in the first place—she was merely pretending.

Nevertheless, there is one instance of Mary displaying a rather unique ability to which all of her classmates— even her detractors—would attest. While she was studying at the academy, there was apparently an incident in which a "lunatic," as they termed it, escaped from a nearby mental institution and ran into the schoolyard wielding a club. The madman seemed bent on harming himself or someone else, and the children had to be evacuated from the area. However, while everyone else scattered and ran back inside, Mary went right up to the individual, took his hand, and convinced him to calm down. Everyone who saw it was amazed—whatever words Mary used to calm the distraught man worked instantly. He was raving mad and ready to beat someone to death one minute, and then completely at peace the next.

Apart from her teachers, Mary's greatest mentor growing up was one of her older brothers, Albert Baker. A brilliant young man in his own right, Albert took great interest in his sister's education and tutored her in many subjects including Hebrew, Greek, and Latin. At this time, Albert had already become a rather prominent lawyer, and he was on his way to ascending the political ladder when a devastating illness took hold. Albert had a condition that rendered him with only one functioning kidney, and when that lone kidney began to fail him his health saw a steep decline. It was actually right after his nomination to a congressional election in 1841 that his health gave out completely. Albert Baker was only 31 years of age, and his death was certainly untimely and unexpected. It would prove to be a severe blow to the family—one that would haunt Mary for the rest of her life.

Shortly after the passing of her brother, Mary would begin to court her first husband, George Washington Glover. Hailing from Concord, New Hampshire, George was a friend of Mary's eldest brother Samuel and had worked with him on construction ventures in the past. Mary had first met George at Samuel's wedding a few years prior, but it wasn't until the early 1840s that they began to date each other in earnest.

The couple would be officially wed on December 10, 1843 when Mary was 22 years old. It was said to have been an extravagant affair with a large number of family and friends arriving to bear witness to and celebrate their day of holy matrimony. Shortly after their marriage ceremony, the young bride left with her husband for

Charleston, South Carolina, where George owned some property.

It was here that Mary first became aware of the evil of slavery in a very real way. As a Northern girl, she had listened to the debates about slavery at dinner table discussions, but it had always an abstract idea that was argued. Now that Mary saw the reality of slavery with her own eyes, it immediately made her the most strident of abolitionists, and she urged her husband to dispense with the practice immediately. The two would argue about this incessantly. At one point, George even tried to convince his wife that freeing his slaves was against state law in South Carolina. Mr. Glover argued that due to a law passed in 1820, it would take a "special act of the legislature" for him even to be allowed to free his slaves. But, no matter what kind of excuse her husband gave, Mary was quick to tell George that to own a human being was to live in a state of sin.

Just a few months into their marriage, Mary and her husband's sojourn in Charleston would be diverted to Wilmington, North Carolina when George was tasked with supplying construction materials for a church that was being built in Haiti. The city happened to be in the midst of a yellow fever outbreak upon their arrival, so George attempted to get the job done as quickly as possible. Unfortunately, he did not get it done quick enough, because George Glover soon came down with the dreaded illness. He would pass away a little over a week later.

During the course of George's illness, the bereaved Mary wasn't even able to stay by her husband's side since his handlers had determined him to be too contagious even for a final farewell. Nevertheless, while on his deathbed, Mr. Glover's mind was on the safety and security of his wife. According to those in attendance, his final request was said to be for the safe passage of his wife back to her father's home in the North.

Chapter Four

The Issue of Slavery

"Each successive period of progress is a period more humane and spiritual. The only logical conclusion is that all is Mind and its manifestation, from the rolling of worlds, in the most subtle ether, to a potato patch."

—Mary Baker Eddy

Although Mary Baker Eddy's husband had passed away after just a few months of marriage, Mary was still carrying a piece of her beloved within her. At the time of George Glover's passing, Mary was already pregnant with his child. This pregnancy gave Mary both great hope and great despair. She was thrilled with the idea of having a baby but anguished by the fact that her child would never get to know its father.

Mary's financial situation was also dire with her husband's passing forcing her once again to depend upon the good graces of her family back in New Hampshire. Fortunately, her parents readily took her in and had her placed right back in the same room that she had claimed as her own before her marriage.

Mary's son, whom she named George Washington Glover, Jr after her deceased husband, was born on September 12, 1844. It is said that Mary was in such a bad state after little George's birth that she could not properly care for the baby. As such, the child was taken to a family friend named Amos Morrison. Morrison's wife had just given birth to twins, but one of the twins had died at childbirth, and so the family agreed to take on George temporarily. Mary, too, was well taken care of and given the chance to recover in peace. She soon regained a small measure of independence and began writing for local publications, even running a small preschool for a few months in 1846.

This same year of 1846 was also when Mary Baker Eddy published a short story called "Emma Clinton, or a Tale of the Frontiers" which was a fictional account of a young woman's tragic marriage. Seemingly based on Mary's life, the main character of the short story had a husband who died of yellow fever just George Glover had in real life. This was a period of reflection and healing, and writing appeared to have a therapeutic effect on Mary as it allowed her to vent some of the powerful currents of emotion she was feeling.

However, it wasn't too long into her stay at her parents' home that Mary was beset with yet another tragedy. Surprising everyone, the health of Mary's mother had rapidly begun to fail her. In November of 1849, the matriarch of the Baker family passed out of this world. At her passing, Mary felt that she had been dealt an unbearable hand. She couldn't believe that her brother, husband, and mother could pass away in such quick succession. Then, Mary was stricken by sorrow again when her new fiancé and childhood friend, John Bartlett, succumbed to disease only three weeks later.

After these recent deaths, Mary found herself suddenly alone in her old childhood home with just her father and her son George. It was indeed a gloomy few months, and the Thanksgiving and Christmas celebrations of 1849 were recorded as the saddest holidays of the family's collective lives. Mary's father, however, was determined not to stay in despair forever and rather quickly found a new wife. Her name was Elizabeth Patterson Duncan. Elizabeth was rather well off considering the money she had inherited from her two previous husbands, but as much as this helped to buoy the spirits of Mary's father, it was of course little consolation to the saddened Mary Baker Eddy. On the contrary, Mark's wedding to Elizabeth in 1850 only served to make Mary's living arrangements more precarious, and soon the family was openly discussing finding a new place for Mary to live.

Initially, Mary seemed to take the move in stride. It was determined that she would move in with her sister Abigail for a while, so as not to strain her father's new attempt at marriage. This part of the arrangement was fine with Mary, but the shock came when it was revealed to her that her son George would not be joining her. George was five years old at this time, and Mary's sister Abigail, who had a four-year-old of her own, was afraid that he would be too much to handle. Thus, it was decided that he would be sent to his old babysitter, a woman named Mahala Sanborn. Ms. Sanborn, who had no children of her own and was past childbearing age, was getting ready to marry a man named Russell Cheney. She and her new husband, without children of their own, agreed to raise young George as their son.

All of this decision making was apparently done without much thought into how Mary, the child's mother, felt about it. When she did get word of their plans, she practically screamed in shock, "What, take my little son?!" Sadly, she did not have much choice in the matter. In those days, a widowed mother without any means of financial support was considered more or less a burden, and it was often up to the family to coordinate ways in which to bear it. Mary knew that she had no real means of income on her own, and so after much discussion between her family members, she finally accepted their proposition. Nevertheless, when the time of their parting came, it was a heartbreaking scene for sure. Mary would later recall how she knelt by George's bed and cried out to God for another way. Still, for the time being, she realized she had to acquiesce. Even through her tears, Mary helped to dress her son and pack his things as she sent him on his way to his new home.

It was in her renewed state of grief while living at her sister's residence, mourning the recent passing her mother and fiancé and the absence of her son, that Mary began to write most prodigiously for a New Hampshire periodical called the *Patriot*. Burying herself in the political debates of the day proved to be therapeutic and served to get Mary's mind off of her sadness and loss. One of the hot topics that Mary wrote about the most was the issue of slavery. Just coming back from the South and witnessing the degradation of slavery herself, Mary was able to provide a first-hand perspective for her Northern reading audience. Along with writing, she also began to teach as a fill-in instructor from time to time at the New Hampshire Conference Seminary.

During this time, the debate over slavery really started to heat up in the United States, and the nation was sliding ever closer to civil war. Several laws were enacted during this period, including the Compromise of 1850 and the infamous Fugitive Slave Act. Things were quickly coming to a head, and soon Mary Baker Eddy would find herself at the very eye of the storm.

Chapter Five

Separated from Her Son

"Experience teaches us that we do not always receive the blessings we ask for in prayer."

—Mary Baker Eddy

Many things in Mary Baker Eddy's life seemed to have occurred by chance. According to her own account, it was indeed by complete chance that she ended up marrying her second husband Daniel Patterson, who was related to Mary's new stepmother Elizabeth Patterson Duncan.

As Mary would later tell the story, it was in late 1852 that she found herself suffering from a terrible toothache and in need of a good dentist. She went to the nearby town of Franklin to visit Dr. Patterson, who was not only a dentist but also an early practitioner of homeopathic medicine. The two apparently hit it off after their encounter and, starting in December of 1852, they began to exchange letters with each other.

A difference between the two that threatened to stand in the way of their relationship, however, was the fact that Daniel was a Baptist, which went against the strict Congregationalist background of the Baker family. As was common of the time, Mary was expected to convert to her husband's religion in the event of their union. This was not something that Mary was willing to do, and she informed to Daniel as much, writing to him, "I have a fixed feeling that to yield my religion to yours I could not."

For this, and other reasons, Mary's father had his doubts about the prospects of his daughter's new love interest but nevertheless, slightly encouraged by the fact that he was a relative of his own wife, he encouraged his daughter to give it a chance. Mary herself would later say that one of the primary motives of her getting married at this point in her life was her search for security. Most importantly, Mary felt that marrying a dentist would provide her with the type of stable home life that was needed for her to reclaim her son. Mary would later recall that before marrying Daniel he had promised to help in this endeavor, going so far as to say that he would make himself the legal guardian of young George. In addition to this, Daniel told Mary's sister Abigail that he believed much of Mary's ailments to be psychosomatic and a result of her separation from her child. Just as he had told Mary, Daniel then proceeded to tell Abigail that he would provide a means for their reunion to occur.

However, as soon as the pair were married, Daniel did a complete about-face and refused to have anything to do with George. At first, he cited Mary's poor health and made the excuse that she had to wait until her health improved before he could commit to bringing her son home with them. But as the days, weeks, months, and years dragged on, this excuse began to wear thin, and it seemed that Daniel had no intention at all of making good on his promise of providing a home for Mary's son. Dr. Patterson was also frequently away from home since his work often required him to make business trips, leaving Mary in continued grief for the loss of her child—a grief which would not be abated until many years later when Mary was eventually reunited with her fully grown and adult son.

While her husband was gone, Mary mostly buried herself in books and prayer during her long stretches alone. A new opportunity then came for Mary in 1856 when she managed to convince her husband to move them to the town of Groton, New Hampshire which brought her closer to where her son was staying with the old nurse Mahala, now wed as Mrs. Russell Cheney. By being in close proximity, Mary hoped to find a way to convince the Cheneys to return her son to her. Back in the mid-nineteenth century, widowed mothers had surprisingly few rights when it came to the raising of their own children. Without a husband to help govern family affairs, the sons and daughters of widows were often very much left to the winds of fate.

According to later accounts, the move closer to her son did indeed breed some familiarity. It is said that shortly after Mary's arrival, her son began to visit her at home. They would sit for hours, and Mary would help George with his schoolwork. But Dr. Patterson, the one who had claimed to be all for the reunion, did not approve and soon banned the child from coming over. Again, he claimed that it was out of respect for Mary's ill health. At first glance, this may seem like the cruel jealousies of a stepfather come to life, but there could be some truth in Daniel's concern all the same. After moving to Groton, much of Mary's old sickness had returned with a vengeance, and she is said to have been bedridden for much of the duration of her stay in this New Hampshire village. So, in some sense, he was telling the truth about her fading health.

Nevertheless, dark happenings were afoot when it came to Mary's son. Dr. Patterson had informed the Cheneys that the child exhausted his mother and ought not be around her. The Cheneys then apparently took this as their cue to fulfill a long-held ambition to go out to Minnesota, thereby ensuring that the child would be away from his meddling mother for good. This trip was carried out in secret in April of 1856. After the child was firmly uprooted and far away from Mary, his foster parents thought it would be a good idea to tell the boy that his mom had died and was already six feet under the ground. They apparently figured that this would end George's yearnings for his mother and allow him to accept his surroundings and cease to seek her out.

Still, even in the face of this subterfuge, both mother and son would continue to pine for each other for many hard years to come. In the end, George would be 34 years old when he finally shook off the cruel bonds of this deception and reunited with his rightful mother.

Chapter Six

Mary during the American Civil War

"I would no more quarrel with a man because of his religion than I would because of his art."

—Mary Baker Eddy

After her son's final departure, Mary's health continued to get worse until she was said to spend several days at a time unmoving and as rigid as a board in bed. She was clearly unable to continue her duties as a housewife and, as such, her husband had hired a housekeeper to help take care of the house. The tenure of this housekeeper, however, would come to an abrupt end.

According to later recollection, the original housekeeper became angry when Mary decided to hire a blind girl named Myra, who had come to her door seeking work. The housekeeper apparently did not take to kindly to the competition and stormed off. Mary would keep Myra in her employment for quite some time, and they would become close friends. Even so, Myra had her difficulties when it came to caring for the ailing Mary Baker Eddy. She would later recall one occasion in particular in which Mary didn't like how she responded to a request and slapped her across the face in a violent rage. This was indeed quite contrary to Mary's normal character, and she showed as much by wrapping her arms around Myra, pleading for her forgiveness. During her difficulties, Mary could become quite short-tempered, but she was always quick to see the wrong of her actions and attempt to right them as expediently as she could, and this incident bears testament to that. Although Myra could still remember the slap years later, all had indeed been forgiven a long time ago.

Mary would be more or less considered an invalid over the next few years with her husband having to devote much of his time to her maintenance. By the late 1850s, the strain of Mary and her husband's home life was then further impacted when Daniel Patterson's dental practice hit a rough patch and started to lose clients. Unable to pay their mortgage any longer, the Pattersons were then forced to find a new home.

They left their former abode in humiliation and shame, a shame that was punctuated by Daniel getting into a fist fight with some of their former neighbors over taking wood he could not pay for as they tried to leave. It was a pitiful scene for sure, but Mary and her husband did manage to escape their burdens in Groton and move to a new home in the hill country of Rumney village.

It was during their tenure here, as America descended into all-out civil war, that Mary's marriage to Daniel Patterson would take the strangest turn of all when her husband was captured by the Confederacy. It all apparently began in early 1862 when Daniel had been directed by the governor of New Hampshire to allocate recently raised funds to Northern sympathizers in the South. This trip took him down dangerous roads right in the middle of the conflict, but Daniel at first did not seem to be too concerned. In fact, on his way past Washington, D.C. he even tried to take a closer look during the Battle of Bull Run. Apparently, he got much too close for comfort and was taken prisoner by troops of the Southern Confederacy. Mary received this news from her sickbed and, spurned to action, began to fire off as many letters as possible in the hope that her husband could be safely returned. As much as later chroniclers have pointed toward the Patterson marriage as a failed one, it is poignant moments such as these that show that there may yet have been some sparks of love in their dying romantic embers after all.

Right around this time, Mary heard that her now teenaged son had enlisted and joined to fight in the American Civil War himself. It seemed a bizarre and frightening moment in time for Mary Baker Eddy to be virtually moribund in her bed while her husband was imprisoned by Confederates and her son was on the battlefield fighting with the Unionists. To say that she felt helpless would be a tremendous understatement. But as has often been the case, it was in this moment of complete helplessness that Mary reached out to the only one she knew she could count on—her God.

Wishing to get up, get better, and reunite with her husband and son, Mary began to scour the Bible for accounts of healing. In these efforts she especially fixated on the scripture that reads, "And these signs shall follow them that believe; they shall lay hands upon the sick and they shall recover." As she meditated upon these words, Mary recalled all of her previous moments with the divine. She remembered how she had been called by the supernatural at a young age. She looked back on the moment in which she had a fever and miraculously recovered. She also remembered how she had managed to calm down the agitated maniac in the schoolyard with a few simple words of grace. In contemplating all of these things, Mary saw that the one common denominator was that she had been in an exalted religious state when the incidents occurred. As such, she began to openly speculate if to these miracles depended upon extreme intensity of faith or whether a calm sense of assurance might not as surely reach God's attention.

It was during this time of intense soul searching that Mary became more well known to other members in her community as word spread of "the good sick lady" that read scripture and prayed for others. Her husband meanwhile was doing his best to stay alive, languishing under Confederate confines in Libby prison in Richmond, Virginia. He would eventually make an escape six months later and after a journey of several weeks return home to his wife. He would find Mary Baker Eddy a dramatically changed woman from the invalid he had left behind.

Chapter Seven

The Birth of Christian Science

"True prayer is not asking God for love; it is learning to love, and to include all mankind in one affection. Prayer is the utilization of the love wherewith He loves us."

—Mary Baker Eddy

Just before Daniel Patterson's capture by the Confederacy, he had reached out to a man named Phineas Parkhurst Quimby. Quimby was known for his ability to encourage healing when all other methods had failed. Worried about Mary's fragile state, Daniel had written Quimby requesting for him to pay a visit to his wife. Quimby apparently did not do house calls, however, and promptly informed Daniel that if he wanted to have his wife healed, he would have to bring her to him. Mary was too sick for such a trip at the time, and then shortly thereafter Daniel was captured by the Confederates.

By October of 1862, despite the hardship, Mary was ready and willing to give Quimby a try. In the care of her elder brother Samuel, she left for Portland, Maine, to see the supposed healer for herself. Mary was 41 years old at the time and was desperately hoping that this visit would render her some sort of aid.

Quimby claimed that Jesus Christ was essentially a kind of metaphysical scientist, and he stated that the healing he practiced "belongs to Wisdom that is above man as man. The Science I try to practice is the Science that was taught eighteen hundred years ago, and has never had a place in the heart of man since; but is in the world, and the world knows it not." According to Quimby, modern doctors were merely misdiagnosing patients and making them sicker. Quimby sought the healing power from within to cure his patients, or as he famously was recorded as saying at the time, "repent all, and be baptized in the Science that will wash away your sins and diseases with your belief."

Mary had already heard much of the happenings centered around this unusual man and was quite impressed before she met him in person. With a tremendous amount of expectation, she came into his company in October of 1862. According to Mary's later account of the encounter, Quimby came out of his inner office to see her, resplendent in his white hair, beard, level brows, and shrewd, penetrating eyes. It was with these eyes that he seemed to keep Mary mesmerized, as he gazed down at his patient.

Looking Mary right in the eye, Quimby commanded her with the authority of a hypnotist to free herself of the bondage of what her family and physicians had told her about her illness. After commanding Mary to meditate on this thought, Quimby then washed his hands in a nearby container of water before using them to vigorously massage her temples. As he did so, he continued to suggest to her that she would be free of her previous baggage and be healed. The next thing Mary knew, the pain had left her, and she did indeed experience an amazing recovery from her previous ailments. But when it came to the reason why Mary had received healing, the two had a decided break in their interpretation. Quimby, who did not profess to be a Christian at the time, seemed to believe that the healing was more due to the power of his suggestion or what he sometimes termed "animal magnetism" rather than anything divine.

Mary, however, saw things quite differently. Mary informed the man in no uncertain terms, "It is not magnetism that does this work, doctor. Your knowledge of God's law, your understanding of the truth which Christ brought into the world and which had been lost for ages." Quimby, prone to grandiose statements, then remarked, "I see what you mean that Christ has come into the world again, but in that case, I must be John and you Jesus."

Saying such things in front of Mary proved to be a fatal mistake as she immediately recoiled in disgust at what she was hearing. She quickly rebuked Quimby, "That is blasphemy." Quimby then backpedaled on his previous statement and corrected, "I didn't mean it so; I don't understand the way you explain your cure. No one before ever believed it was divine truth that operated through me. They have said I healed through some mysterious force in myself. I have told them it was healthy electrical currents together with my Wisdom that I imparted which effected the cure. But the faith in Christ which you declare enables me to heal I have not."

Mary was adamant that what had transpired was simply God working through Quimby—whether he realized it or not. Soon thereafter she instructed him, "You should understand, Dr. Quimby, much better than I that this is not your magnetism or your wisdom but God's truth. I try to understand my cure every day, but I am still confused. You should make clear statements for your patient's sake, not in scribbled notes, but in a developed argument summed up in a treatise."

Here Mary was combining her two great talents—her knack for framing religious argument and her ability to record those arguments in writing. Quimby had up until that point only the vaguest of ideology attached to his healings and had indeed only produced a few "scribbled notes" as to what he believed to be the true source of his healing powers. Mary was now advising him to attach a belief system to his routine.

Quimby at first tried to protest her rigid formula, stating, "I do not understand entirely what I do, so how can I make the patient understand?" To which Mary immediately replied, "But there can be no science of health until the laws can be stated. If this is a philosophy it can be reduced to philosophic arguments. This is a very spiritual doctrine, the eternal years of God are with it, and it must be stated so that it will stand firm as the Rock of Ages."

It was on the heels of these heady words from Mary Baker Eddy that Christian Science as we know it was truly born.

Chapter Eight

On the Brink of Death

"Give up the belief that mind is, even temporarily, compressed within the skull, and you will quickly become more manly or womanly. You will understand yourself and your Maker better than before."

—Mary Baker Eddy

After her session with Quimby, Mary's relatives were amazed to see her return to what had been a long-lost sense of normalcy. But when friends and family tried to challenge the source of her recovery by stating that Quimby was a nothing more than a hypnotist, she would vigorously argue against them, stating her belief that he was a man of God.

Soon thereafter Mary picked up her pen and even trumpeted these beliefs in letter to the *Portland Evening Courier* in which she expressed her appreciation of Quimby's healing acumen. Many who read the letter failed to see what had captivated Mary so much about the man as most saw him as nothing more than a hypnotist at best and a charlatan at worst.

Yet Mary kept right on singing Quimby's praises, and upon returning to her sister Abigail's house her incessant chatter finally perked her sister's interest. Abigail determined to pay a visit to Quimby herself to see what all of the chatter was about. In stark contrast to Mary, Abigail left her session with Quimby extremely disappointed. Instead of finding a mind with a God-given gift of healing as Mary had described, she merely found her former prejudices about Quimby realized. After just a few minutes with the man, Abigail quickly decided that he was indeed a charlatan who used the power of suggestion and hypnotism to influence the minds of his patients. But even so, she was happy that her sister was feeling better, no matter what the actual cause of her deliverance may have been.

Mary had turned over a new leaf, and she was now ready to put her renewed energy and focus to good use. Her husband at this point was still imprisoned by the Confederates with no release date in sight. Seeking to get him back home, Mary began to intercede on his behalf. In these efforts, she took written requests for his release from New Hampshire's governor and traveled to Washington, D.C. to deliver them to President Abraham Lincoln. These efforts would soon become stalled in Washington bureaucracy, however, and in reality, the only way her husband was freed was under his own power. He managed to escape from his captors in a daring jailbreak. Soon Daniel Patterson returned home, penniless, threadbare, and emaciated but otherwise unharmed. Despite their previous differences, Mary was happy to have her husband back once again.

Upon his return, Daniel attempted to set up shop in Massachusetts, but he had trouble keeping clients. In addition to this, there were several rumors circulating Daniel, suggesting that he was seeing other women on the side. Indeed, as much as Mary had sought his recovery, with her husband's return came a reintroduction of a lot of the same problems that had plagued her and Daniel's entire married lives. As these old cycles of iniquity returned, so did Mary Baker Eddy's physical ailments. Mary tried to persevere, but a tragic accident would seemingly send her right to death's door.

On February 3, 1866, Mary slipped and fell on the ice while walking through town. The fall was bad enough that she sustained internal injury. She was taken to a home of nearby friends, and a doctor was called to care for her. During the night as they struggled to stabilize her condition, Mary was given morphine and other drugs to ease the terrible pain that she had endured. Mary would pull through, and although some ascribe her healing as being miraculous, her doctor always maintained that it was simply medicine and bed rest that helped aid in her recovery.

Mary, however, was convinced that this was indeed another case of divine intervention in her life and would never forget it. Although bedridden, she had reached into herself for the answer to her struggle. As she would put it at the time, "In the year 1866 I discovered the Christ Science, or divine laws of life, and named it Christian Science. God had been graciously fitting me, during many years, for the reception of a final revelation of the absolute divine Principle of scientific being and healing."

Mary had been ravaged by sickness and disease but came back a full-fledged Christian Scientist. She would take it upon herself to develop this science into a religious movement over the coming years, culminating in the publication of her most important work, *Science and Health with Key to the Scriptures*, in 1875 and the official creation of Church of Christ, Scientist in 1879.

Chapter Nine

A Matter of Faith

"Happiness is spiritual, born of truth and love. It is unselfish; therefore it cannot exist alone, but requires all mankind to share it."

—Mary Baker Eddy

In 1866, Mary had a series of what she perceived to be divine revelations from on high. Meanwhile, her husband Daniel Patterson was drifting further and further away. There have been many who have lambasted Patterson as an unfit husband for his abandonment; he was by this point no doubt weary of his wife's eccentricities.

After Mary became an adherent to Quimby and began to morph his teachings into her own, it seems that Patterson saw something in her that he did not like and sought for the exit door. He found his exit in the form of one of his dental patients. Like him, she too was already married to someone else, but casting the sanctity of marriage to the side, they ran off together, leaving their respective spouses behind. This affair didn't last for long, and it was actually Mr. Patterson's new partner who first came to Mary, begging for her forgiveness. The woman apparently felt genuinely bad for the disturbance of both their marriages. Citing the fact that Daniel often brought up Mary's religiousness, she figured that Mary could serve as some kind of intercessor between her and her own husband. Mary, not showing any sign of wrath or rancor, readily obliged. Amazingly, she managed to bring the husband back on good terms with his renegade wife, and the two were able to resume their married life in due course.

But as magnanimous as she was in patching up the relations between her rival and her spouse, Mary was not quite so forgiving when it came to her own husband. Rather than taking him back, Mary gave Daniel the cold shoulder. It is said that he returned, begging her for mercy, but she refused to give it to him. Mary bluntly informed him, "The same roof cannot shelter us. You may come in, certainly, if you desire, but in that case I must go elsewhere." This was obviously her way of saying that whether they officially divorced or not, they would not live together as a couple again. Daniel Patterson would never be the same after this, and for all of Mary's talk of healing and redemption, he would die alone, a spurned and shattered man.

Mary's mentor that led her down the path of Christian Science, Phineas Quimby, passed away in 1866, and so in the ensuing years the path was wide open for Mary to pursue her conviction that the science of Christ could bring about all manner of healing and restoration for the human condition. Mary's own personal life meanwhile was in constant upheaval. Still largely dependent on the generosity of others for sustenance, she found herself bouncing from boarding house to boarding house and several intermittent stays with friends in between. At one point, her sister Abigail had offered to let Mary stay with her, but it was only on the condition that she drop some of her more eccentric behavior. Mary refused.

She continued to drift from person to person among her growing circle of friends. Although her lifestyle was chaotic, it was fruitful. Like some sort of philosophical bee going from ideological flower to ideological flower, Mary began to pollinate several different ideas among the intellectuals that she was staying with. Among a wide variety of spiritualists, mentalists, and fundamentalist Christians, Mary continued to refine and revise the spiritual awakening that had begun under the auspices of Phineas Quimby.

By the summer of 1867, Mary had grown weary of her life as a drifter and decided to return to her childhood home. Adding to her sadness over Quimby's death in the previous year, her father Mark Baker had also succumbed to his final end in October of 1866. Due to the many tumultuous events in her life in late 1866, she was unable to fully process the loss. For that reason, Mary determined to make the trek back to where she grew up in Tilton, New Hampshire in the summer of 1867. Here memories of several momentous events in her life came flooding back. She would walk through the garden and think of times that she had passed strolling through it with her local pastor, watering flowers while cultivating her religious faith.

Other places at the old homestead reminded her of when she left to get married to her first husband, George

Glover. Still more triggers would make her sadly reminisce about having her baby—the son that she would never really get to know for herself. Now firmly in middle age, all of these memories of her youth were far away from her, yet at the same time quite close to her consciousness.

Another reason for staying on at the old family farm was to see her sibling, also named George, who had just dropped in after departing from where he resided in Baltimore. Seeing her older brother George was a moment of sadness as well because in later years he had become sick and blind from a degenerative illness. Mary, taking her faith to heart, attempted to engage her ailing brother with her healing sessions, but George refused to take part and died shortly thereafter.

Mary was doubly saddened that yet another family member had passed and that even after all of her work helping others, she was not able to render any aid in the slightest. After George's passing, Mary went to see her sister—a visit that proved to be melancholic at best. At this stage in her life, Mary was often resented and sometimes even ridiculed for what her family felt were beliefs that strayed too far away from the mainstream.

During her return home, Mary would later recall feeling something akin to how Christ must have felt when he went back to his hometown of Nazareth. According to scriptures, even after his several healings and raising people from the dead, the people that knew him from his childhood openly scoffed, "Is not this the carpenter's son?" Mary realized that in even in the face of miracles, the common familiarity of the past could breed contempt and certainly a large amount of skepticism. In a similar vein, her old friends and neighbors often wondered, "Isn't this Mary—the invalid?" They couldn't quite grasp the transformation that this formerly sick and bedridden woman had made. According to the Bible, Jesus, despite his great miracles in the surrounding Judean territories, could not heal so much as a headache in Nazareth, simply because the people were unwilling to have faith and refused to believe. Mary, in her own personal understanding of the necessity of faith, understood this phenomenon quite well. Even Phineas Quimby—who although not attributing healing to God but the power of the human mind—knew that if he could not convince his subjects that they would be healed, they would not be healed.

The great lack of belief in Mary's abilities was distressing as she revisited her old childhood haunts, but during her tenure in Tilton she did find one who chose to believe. She was at her sister Martha's house when Martha's 21-year-old daughter Ellen suddenly fell ill. According to later accounts, the girl had developed a dangerous abscess and grew sicker and sicker by the hour. Mary rushed to her bedside. After just a brief word and prayer with the girl, to the astonishment of her family, Ellen rose from her bed and joined them at the kitchen table for dinner. No one wanted to believe that their relative Mary was a healer, yet they could not dispute what they had seen with their own eyes. For Mary Baker Eddy, it was always just a matter of faith.

Conclusion

Although Phineas Quimby had developed a dramatic practice of healing during his lifetime, he had failed to cultivate acolytes to carry on his work after he was gone. After Quimby's death, Mary Baker Eddy was virtually alone as the sole inheritor of his efforts. Mary was determined not to make the same mistakes as her mentor, however, and began to slowly cobble together a group of followers.

Among these early followers was Asa Gilbert Eddy, the man who would become Mary's third husband in 1877. Mary's core group of devotees are what would later become the Church of Christ, Scientist, founded in 1879. Members of this church group would travel far and wide, spreading their doctrinal beliefs and practice of faith healing.

As the reputation of her movement began to build, Mary then founded the Massachusetts Metaphysical College in 1881. This school is said to have instructed over 800 students by the time Mary shut the doors of the seminary in 1889. From here Mary went on to pastor her new church in Boston, called The Mother Church, which opened its doors in 1894.

Mary, with her long history as a writer and journalist, was still active on the literary front as well, and in 1898, she created the Christian Science Publishing Society. This would then lead to what could be arguably one of her greatest accomplishment, the founding of the long-praised periodical publication *The Christian Science Monitor*, which was established ten years later in 1908 when Mary Baker Eddy was 87 years old. Active to this day, *CSM* has won seven Pulitzer Prizes along with many other press awards.

At the end of her life, Mary Baker Eddy had managed to rise above great difficulties in order to attain tremendous achievements. When she passed away on December 8, 1910, at age 89, Mary Baker Eddy could rest assured knowing that she had indeed changed the world. Her legacy lives on within the 1,700 modern-day Christian Science churches which are spread across more than 75 countries. Many of the periodicals and magazines she founded are still in circulation, educating readers on the doctrine and teachings of one of America's most fascinating religious leaders, Mary Baker Eddy.

Printed in Great Britain
by Amazon